Most Christians want more intimacy with Christ and to see more of His power revealed in our lives, but we're often unwilling to do what it takes. *Fasting* unveils practical steps and a clear understanding to guide us into a deeper level of intimacy with our heavenly Father.

—CRAIG GROESCHEL
SENIOR PASTOR OF LIFECHURCH.TV

fasting
STUDY GUIDE

fasting
STUDY GUIDE

Jentezen Franklin

Charisma
HOUSE
A STRANG COMPANY

Most Strang Communications Book Group products are available at special quantity discounts for bulk purchase for sales promotions, premiums, fund-raising, and educational needs. For details, write Strang Communications Book Group, 600 Rinehart Road, Lake Mary, Florida 32746, or telephone (407) 333-0600.

Fasting Study Guide by Jentezen Franklin
Published by Charisma House
A Strang Company
600 Rinehart Road
Lake Mary, Florida 32746
www.strangbookgroup.com

Design Director: Bill Johnson
Cover design by Justin Evans

Library of Congress Cataloging-in-Publication Data:

Franklin, Jentezen, 1962-
  Fasting study guide / by Jentezen Franklin. -- 1st ed.
    p. cm.
  ISBN 978-1-59979-768-7
  1. Fasting--Religious aspects--Christianity--Textbooks. I. Title.
  BV5055.F735 2009
  248.4'7--dc22

                                        2009020833

First Edition

09 10 11 12 13 — 9 8 7 6 5 4 3 2 1
Printed in Canada

Contents

Session One

Fasting for Your Breakthrough

As the deer pants for the water brooks, so pants my soul for You, O God. My soul thirsts for God, for the living God. When shall I come and appear before God? My tears have been my food day and night, while they continually say to me, "Where is your God?"

—PSALM 42:1–3

Introduction

Questions to get you thinking

1. Fasting is just one of the threefold cords of spiritual life. What are the other two?

_____

_____

_____

2. What do you understand the purpose of fasting to be?

_____

_____

_____

3. What is the spiritual breakthrough that you want to be the result of your fast?

_____

_____

_____

Play Session One of the DVD

Notes from the DVD segment

Fasting: the basics

_____

_____

_____

Before you begin…

     Prepare spiritually

_____

_____

_____

     Prepare physically

_____

_____

_____

Decide what to fast

_____

_____

_____

Decide how long to fast

_____

_____

_____

Start with a clear goal

_____

_____

_____

Types of fasts

Full fast

_____

_____

_____

Partial fast

_____

_____

_____

Daniel fast

_____

_____

_____

Corporate fast

_____

_____

_____

How to end your fast

_____

_____

_____

DVD action points

Simply stated, biblical fasting is refraining from food for a spiritual purpose. Fasting has always been a normal part of a relationship with God.

1. The video segment listed several reasons for fasting and discussed how we can continue to experience the blessings of fasting. Which ones do you feel best apply to your own life and decision to fast?

_____

_____

_____

2. How can you prepare physically and spiritually to be ready to fast?

_____

_____

_____

3. The video segment talked about several different kinds of fasts. Describe each one:

Full fast

_____

_____

_____

Partial fast

_____

_____

_____

Daniel fast

_____

_____

_____

Corporate fast

_____

_____

_____

What God's Word tells us

Fasting is for everyone

During the years that Jesus walked this earth, He devoted time to teaching His disciples the principles of the kingdom of God, principles that conflict with those of this world. In the Beatitudes, specifically in Matthew 6, Jesus provided the pattern by which each of us is to live as a child of God. That pattern addressed three specific duties of a Christian: giving, praying, and fasting. Jesus said, "*When* you give…," "*When* you pray…," and "*When* you fast." He made it clear that fasting, like giving and praying, was a normal part of Christian life. As much attention should be given to fasting as is given to giving and to praying.

1. In Matthew 17, Matthew tells the story of a father who had a demon-possessed son. When he brought his son to the disciples, they could not cure him. When the boy was brought to Jesus, he was instantly cured. When the disciples asked Jesus why they could not cure him, Jesus gave them the answer found in Matthew 17:20–21. In your own words, explain why Jesus said the disciples failed.

   _____

   _____

   _____

2. In Matthew 6 we learn that God delights in giving rewards when we give, pray, and fast. Read the story

of Daniel's partial fast when he refused to eat the rich food offered him in the palace, choosing to eat only vegetables instead, and explain how God rewarded him for his faithfulness to his fast.

_____

_____

_____

3. In Genesis 2:8–9, 16–17, we discover what happened when Adam and Eve allowed themselves to be ruled by "King Stomach" and failed to dethrone that "dictator within." Read the story, and explain what happened.

_____

_____

_____

Discover

On pages 27–28 of *Fasting*, I give three reasons why it is a good practice to start the year with a fast. What are these three reasons, and how could each reason help you begin the journey to a spiritual breakthrough?

Reflecting on what I learned

If you have read my book *Fasting: Opening the door to a deeper, more intimate, more powerful relationship with God,* by now you are beginning to realize how crucial the practice of fasting is in the life of every believer. I write:

> As a part of that threefold cord of normal Christian duties, why is it so often overlooked? I believe the primary reason is one that has plagued mankind since the dawn of creation.
>
> You see, fasting means crucifying what I refer to as "King Stomach." And in case you don't know who King Stomach is, just move this book out of the way, look down, and introduce yourself. You've probably already heard him rumble in disagreement a time or two since you began reading this book!
>
> Every year our entire congregation at Free Chapel Worship Center participates in a twenty-one-day fast. Without fail, folks share with me that they feel like eating everything in sight that last week or so before beginning the fast. But that's OK. Once you make that decision to fast, even if it's just for a day, God sees the desire of your heart. He will provide you with the grace to endure and see the breakthroughs you need come to pass. However, you will have to choose to dethrone that "dictator within."

As you prepare to begin your fast, use this period of reflection to determine how you will dethrone "King Stomach" from his throne in your life. Remember that with just one meal (a piece of fruit, at that), Adam and Eve went from a place in God's presence to fearfully hiding from Him.

1. Make a list and reflect on times when your own desires (it may be for food or drink, for worldly pleasures such as activities or time with friends, or even idleness before a TV) have kept you from spending time with God in prayer and meditation.

    _____

    _____

    _____

2. Remember how Esau's lust for food and instant gratification was more important to him than the plan and destiny God had for his life? We live in a day of "instant gratification." List three ways that your own desire to be instantly gratified interfered with something that you know was God's plan for your life for that moment or day. What are the factors that have caused you to fail to move forward in what you know is God's destiny for your life?

    _____

    _____

    _____

3. Memories of "what used to be" (Num. 11:4–6) caused the Israelites to complain about the path God was leading them on to the Promised Land. God had

supernatural blessings to pour out on them, but they preferred their carnal appetites. What carnal appetites do you need to dethrone? What are the supernatural blessings you want to see God pour out upon your life?

_____

_____

_____

Let's pray about it

In *Fasting*, I write:

> I want you to understand that there are some "promised lands" and some "promises" that God has for you. In fact, we have an entire book of promises, but some of them will never be realized as long as King Stomach rules your appetite and controls your life. God had supernatural blessings to pour out on the Israelites in the wilderness, but they preferred their carnal appetites. Likewise, God wants to pour out supernatural blessings in our lives, but they will never be realized if we are not willing to seek Him in fasting and prayer.

Begin by praying aloud Psalm 139:1–7, 23–24:

> O Lord, You have searched me and known me.
> You know my sitting down and my rising up;
> You understand my thought afar off.
> You comprehend my path and my lying down,

And are acquainted with all my ways.
For there is not a word on my tongue,
But behold, O LORD, You know it altogether.
You have hedged me behind and before,
And laid Your hand upon me.
Such knowledge is too wonderful for me;
It is high, I cannot attain it.

Where can I go from Your Spirit?
Or where can I flee from Your presence?...

Search me, O God, and know my heart;
Try me, and know my anxieties;
And see if there is any wicked way in me,
And lead me in the way everlasting.

Pray about the factors you listed in the personal reflection time that have hindered you from moving forward in God's plan for your life. Make a personal commitment to eliminate as many of these distractions as possible from your life during your fast.

For your journey

There is never a convenient time to fast. In our busy lives there is always a holiday, birthday, office lunch, or something that creates a bump in the road, so we talk ourselves out of beginning a fast. So my advice to you, based on personal experience, is to just jump in and do it and everything else will take care of itself! If you have never fasted before, just do it for one day and you will see what I mean.

Digging deeper in God's Word

Read each of the following illustrations of Bible characters who learned to dethrone King Stomach through a time of fasting and prayer. Jot down notes from each story to help you in your own personal time of fasting and prayer.

1. Moses received the Ten Commandments during a forty-day fast (Exod. 34:27–28).

   _____

   _____

   _____

2. Esther called for all the Jews in her city to fast three days with her before she made a plea to the king to spare the Jews from Haman's death plot (Esther 4–7).

   _____

   _____

   _____

3. Hannah "wept and did not eat" because of her distress at not being able to bear a child. God heard her plea, and the prophet Samuel was born (1 Sam. 1).

_____

_____

_____

4. Nehemiah fasted and prayed because of his sorrow over the broken and burned walls of Jerusalem that needed to be rebuilt. As a result, God called and equipped him to lead in the rebuilding of the walls (Neh. 1–6).

_____

_____

_____

My prayer journal

Each year, I encourage believers to join with the members of my church as they fast and pray for twenty-one days. If in twenty-one days you can be a new person, why go the rest of your life feeling sick, weak, overweight, and run down? Why not take a radical step of faith? We have only one life to give to God—let's get control of our bodies and go for God with the best we have!

As you commit to a period of fasting and study using this study guide and DVD, you will have thirty-five days for stepping out in faith through prayer and fasting. No matter how many of these days you determine will be "fast days," use every day as a period of growing closer to God through prayer.

Get a copy of my twenty-one-day *Fasting Journal*, and commit to working through its information and steps as an additional step of faith during your thirty-five-day study with this book. You will be glad you did!

If you do not have a copy of the *Fasting Journal*, add notes from your personal journey on the lines below.

_____

_____

_____

_____

_____

_____

_____

_____

_____

_____

_____

_____

_____

_____

_____

_____

_____

_____

_____

I have not departed from the commandment
of His lips; I have treasured the words of His
mouth more than my necessary food.

—JOB 23:12—

Session Two

Every Assignment
Has a Birthplace

My sheep hear My voice, and I know them, and they follow Me. And I give them eternal life, and they shall never perish; neither shall anyone snatch them out of My hand.

—John 10:27–28

Introduction

Questions to get you thinking

1. I spoke about a planned period of fasting that I have observed since the age of seventeen. During one three-day fast, I was given God's assignment for my life. What spiritual lessons have you learned from a previous fasting experience?

_____

_____

_____

2. We will be discovering how to more accurately find God's will for our lives in today's video segment. What specific spiritual revelation do you hope to receive as you fast and pray?

_____

_____

_____

Play Session Two of the DVD

Notes from the DVD segment

Fasting clears your ears to hear what God is saying.

_____

_____

_____

Fasting prepares the way for God to do amazing things in your life.

_____

_____

_____

Fasting helps to confirm God's will in your life.

_____

_____

_____

The first time fasting is mentioned in the Bible revealed God's choice of a wife for Jacob.

_____

_____

_____

DVD action points

> God has specific assignments for your life. I am convinced that we will never walk in the perfect will of God until we seek Him through fasting.

1. Every assignment, every call of God, every direction from Him starts somewhere. God has specific assignments for your life. What are the assignments and callings that you know right now that God has placed upon your life? What steps have you taken previously to move forward in the callings that God has given to you?

_____

_____

_____

2. I told you how I received my assignment to preach after prayer and fasting. Briefly tell how God has revealed

something to you. How do you hope to hear God's voice better at the end of this period of fasting and praying?

_____

_____

_____

3. In Acts 10:9 we learned that Peter had fasted and prayed on a rooftop for three days. What dream did God give Peter that gave him his next assignment in ministry?

_____

_____

_____

4. I helped you to see the step-by-step way God led me to pastor our church in Orange County, California. Has there been a situation in your life where God ordered your steps? Where would you like for God to reveal His step-by-step leading to help you?

_____

_____

_____

What God's Word tells us

The significance of forty

Throughout the Bible, the number forty represents cleansing and purifying. Jesus didn't fast twenty-five days or even thirty-eight days. "He was there in the wilderness forty days, tempted by Satan, and was with the wild beasts; and the angels ministered to Him" (Mark 1:13).

Other examples of the importance of forty days can be found throughout the Bible. Read each Bible story below, and jot down the spiritual importance of each forty-day period:

1. It rained for forty days and forty nights during Noah's flood (Gen. 7).

_____

_____

_____

2. The twelve Israelite spies searched the land for forty days, and the children of Israel wandered in the wilderness for forty years (Num. 13–14).

_____

_____

_____

3. After fleeing from Jezebel, Elijah went forty days without food after an angel fed him and watched over him as he rested. During that time, he spoke with God and received new direction (1 Kings 19).

_____

_____

_____

4. Jesus fasted for forty days and forty nights in the wilderness before He was tempted three times by Satan (Matt. 4).

_____

_____

_____

Discover

> Do you want God to tell you what you need to do
> at this time in your life? Fast, worship, and seek Him.
> When you honor and worship God by presenting
> your body as a living sacrifice through fasting, you
> too will know His assignments for your life.

Reflecting on what I learned

If we are not careful, we can allow life to get us into the same old ruts and routines without even realizing it. Our relationships with the Lord can suffer the same fate. When we don't do what it takes to stay sharp and sensitive to the Holy Spirit, our praise, worship, offerings, and even preaching can become heartless routines to God. As a believer, you can pray, read your Bible, and go to church week after week and still be losing sight of your first love. It is not that you don't love the Lord, but the business of life can bring you to the point of losing your freshness, your enthusiasm, and your sensitivity to His Spirit and what pleases Him.

That's why God said to Israel, "If I were hungry, I would not tell you; for the world is Mine, and all its fullness" (Ps. 50:12). God owns the cattle on a thousand hills. He does not need our routines. He does not savor heartless activity. He does not want our "leftovers" when He can get "fed" elsewhere. True worship that comes from our hearts feeds Him and satisfies Him; it is something He desires—and deserves. Our religiosity of going through the motions once a week does not please Him as much as our obedience to His Word.

Fasting is a constant means of renewing yourself spiritually. The discipline of fasting breaks you out of the world's routine. It is a form of worship. Offering your body to God as a living sacrifice is holy and pleasing to God (Rom. 12:1). The discipline of fasting will humble you, remind you of your dependency on God, and bring you back to your first love. It causes the roots of your relationship with Jesus to go deeper.

1. In chapter 6, "God's Coming to Dinner?" of *Fasting*, we discover: "When you take steps to break out of the ordinary and worship God as He deserves, you will begin to see facets of His being you never knew existed." How can you break out of your *rituals* for worshiping God and spending time in His presence? What specific steps can you take to move from casual, disinterested worship to passionately worshiping and magnifying God as He deserves?

   _____

   _____

   _____

2. In Psalm 34:3 we are told to "magnify the LORD." Luke 1:46–55 is Mary's song, in which she magnifies the Lord for the specific ways He had ministered to her and to others. Read Mary's song, and write your own song to magnify God in your own way:

   _____

   _____

   _____

3. God assures us in 2 Chronicles 7:14 that no matter how dark the hour or no matter what is going on in our lives, our nation, or the world, His promises are true, and He rules and reigns above all these things. Spend some time reflecting on those things in your community, nation, and world for which you will pray and seek God's face for healing and restoration. List those for which you will commit to fast and pray:

_____

_____

_____

Let's pray about it

In Psalm 34, David said, "I sought the LORD, and He heard me, and delivered me from all my fears" (v. 4). God will hear you when you set your heart to worship Him. When you magnify the Lord, you shrink the supposed power of your enemy, the devil. The greatest thing you can do in the midst of a battle is magnify the Lord.

Begin by praying aloud:

> I will bless the LORD at all times: his praise shall continually be in my mouth. My soul shall make her boast in the LORD: the humble shall hear thereof, and be glad. O magnify the LORD with me, and let us exalt his name together. I sought the LORD, and he heard me, and delivered me from all my fears....
>
> The angel of the LORD encampeth round about them that fear him, and delivereth them. O taste and see that the LORD is good: blessed is the man that trusteth in him.

O fear the LORD, ye his saints: for there is no want to them that fear him....

The eyes of the LORD are upon the righteous, and his ears are open unto their cry. The face of the LORD is against them that do evil, to cut off the remembrance of them from the earth. The righteous cry, and the LORD heareth, and delivereth them out of all their troubles. The LORD is nigh unto them that are of a broken heart; and saveth such as be of a contrite spirit.

Many are the afflictions of the righteous: but the LORD delivereth him out of them all. He keepeth all his bones: not one of them is broken. Evil shall slay the wicked: and they that hate the righteous shall be desolate. The LORD redeemeth the soul of his servants: and none of them that trust in him shall be desolate.

—PSALM 34:1–4, 7–9, 15–22, KJV

Now spend a few moments of *praise time* by magnifying the Lord for the specific things He has done in your own life in the past.

List some of the things in your life or world that cause you to fear. Pray about these fears specifically, focusing on:

- "The angel of the LORD encampeth round about [you]."
- "Taste and see that the LORD is good."
- "Blessed is the man that trusteth in him."
- "The eyes of the Lord are upon the righteous."
- "His ears are open unto their cry."

For your journey

Because of Jesus, you and I can take hold of God's promises to protect us, to provide for all our needs, and to cover us in His love, mercy, and grace. He is our *El Shaddai*. He shows Himself strong on our behalf, but He also tenderly takes us unto Himself and shows us kindness. Meditate on these verses of Scripture today, relating to the divine protection of our loving Father:

You yourselves have seen what I did to Egypt, and how I carried you on eagles' wings and brought you to myself. Now if you obey me fully and keep my covenant, then out of all nations you will be my treasured possession.
—EXODUS 19:4–5, NIV—

For you have been my refuge, a strong tower against the foe. I long to dwell in your tent forever and take refuge in the shelter of your wings. For you have heard my vows, O God; you have given me the heritage of those who fear your name.
—PSALM 61:3–5, NIV—

As a mother comforts her child, so will I comfort you; and you will be comforted over Jerusalem.
—ISAIAH 66:13, NIV—

What is God saying to you today about His protection?

Digging deeper in God's Word

David was a man after God's heart. He was a man who fasted often, and not just from food. As a youth, he was often in the fields alone with just the sheep and his God. After he was anointed king, he spent many days running for his life. David wrote Psalm 34 while alone and on the run from Saul in the land of the Philistines. But David stirred himself to worship God even in those conditions, proclaiming, "His praise shall continually be in my mouth" (v. 1), and "taste and see that the LORD is good" (v. 8). A routine worshiper in those circumstances would have been totally overwhelmed. But David knew that to worship God was to magnify God. His invitation to all of us to "magnify the LORD with [him]" (v. 3) still stands open today.

Read each of the Scripture portions from David in the chart below and complete the two columns, listing: (1) David's specific praise to God, and (2) how you will praise God in a similar circumstance in your own life:

Psalm	David's Specific Praise	How You Will Praise God
Psalm 3:1–8		
Psalm 8:1–9		
Psalm 14:1–7		
Psalm 26:1–12		
Psalm 32:1–11		
Psalm 53:1–6		
Psalm 101:1–8		

My prayer journal

Continue working through the *Fasting Journal* as an additional step of faith during your thirty-five-day study with this book. You will be glad you did! If you do not have a copy of the *Fasting Journal*, read the story of Jesus's visit with the woman at the well in Samaria in John 4. After her encounter with Jesus, this woman ran back to her town, telling everyone, "Come, see a Man who told me all things that I ever did" (v. 29).

On the lines below, journal the things that God has revealed to you through this second session on fasting. How have you learned to magnify God to others?

_____

_____

_____

_____

_____

_____

_____

_____

_____

_____

_____

_____

_____

_____

_____

Bless the LORD, O my soul;
And all that is within me, bless His holy name!
Bless the LORD, O my soul,
And forget not all His benefits:
Who forgives all your iniquities,
Who heals all your diseases,
Who redeems your life from destruction,
Who crowns you with lovingkindness
and tender mercies,
Who satisfies your mouth with good things,
So that your youth is renewed like the eagle's.

—PSALM 103:1–5—

Session Three

Rewarded Openly

"Hear me, O Judah and you inhabitants of Jerusalem: Believe in the LORD your God, and you shall be established; believe His prophets, and you shall prosper." And when he had consulted with the people, he appointed those who should sing to the LORD, and who should praise the beauty of holiness, as they went out before the army and were saying: "Praise the LORD, for His mercy endures forever."

—2 CHRONICLES 20:20–21

Introduction

Questions to get you thinking

1. When was the last time you really heard God speak to you about an answer for which you were seeking Him?

_____

_____

_____

2. Have the daily challenges, obstacles, and circumstances of your life become so massive in your mind that you see only the mountain—and cannot see the fertile valley beyond?

_____

_____

_____

3. Have your own complaints, pleas, cries, and questions to God about your problems grown so loud that they have become "sounding brass or a clanging cymbal" (1 Cor. 13:1)?

_____

_____

_____

Play Session Three of the DVD

Notes from the DVD segment

Health and healing will follow fasting.

_____

_____

_____

Fasting can break unhealthy eating habits.

_____

_____

_____

Fasting breaks financial chains and brings financial resources.

_____

_____

_____

Fasting gives you more of God.

_____

_____

_____

When you fast, everything slows down.

_____

_____

_____

Fasting gives you authority over Satan.

_____

_____

_____

DVD action points

> We must arrive at the place where we are desperate for God again. Your faithfulness during this time of fasting and prayer will bring supernatural blessings and release the power of God to overcome any situation.

1. I told you how eager I was to spend more and more time with Cherise when we were dating because we were lovesick for each other. Are you lovesick for God? Are you eager to spend time with Him? How can you spend more time with Him?

   _____

   _____

   _____

2. Are you experiencing a time when you just need to stop the busyness of your life to spend more time in His presence? What busyness keeps you from that now? How are you willing to change to have more time for God?

   _____

   _____

   _____

3. In Psalm 34:4, David said he sought the Lord and the Lord delivered him from his fears and enemies. The greatest thing you can do in the midst of a battle is magnify the Lord. What are the fears and enemies you are facing? How can you magnify God to make Him bigger than your fears and enemies?

_____

_____

_____

4. Mark 9:28–29 tells the story of the father with a boy possessed by a demonic spirit. What was the reason Jesus gave His disciples to explain why they could not heal him? Are there demonic strongholds in your life that you have not been set free from? Will you commit this time of prayer and fasting to secure your freedom from the devil's hold?

_____

_____

_____

What God's Word tells us

Praise pushes back the enemy

You wear depression and oppression like a garment. It shrouds you in darkness and despair. It is a heavy garment that continues to drag you down. It keeps you from lifting your head and from raising your hands in praise to God. Heaviness drains worship out of your life. But praise pushes back the enemy!

The story of King Jehoshaphat in 2 Chronicles 20 is a wonderful example of how praise pushes back the enemy. Begin this Bible exploration section by reading that chapter. We will look closer at how King Jehoshaphat learned this important lesson.

1. Jehoshaphat had determined that he would serve God. We learn that he "sought the God of his father, and walked in His commandments" (2 Chron. 17:4). As a result, "Therefore the LORD established the kingdom in his hand; and all Judah gave presents to Jehoshaphat, and he had riches and honor in abundance" (v. 5). He had gotten rid of all the idols to false gods in Judah and sent Levitical teachers to instruct the people in the ways of God (v. 6). He had also set judges over the kingdom and instructed them to judge courageously, assuring them that God would be with them. He was doing everything right!

   In spite of that, he was told: "A great multitude is coming against you from beyond the sea" (2 Chron. 20:2). Have you ever felt like Jehoshaphat felt at that moment? "And Jehoshaphat feared" (v. 3). Describe a time in your life when it seemed as though you were doing everything right, and in spite of that, a huge challenge came your way that caused you great fear.

_____

_____

_____

2. But the story doesn't stop there for Jehoshaphat. The Bible indicates that his fear was only momentary— only as long as it takes to stick a comma in the story. The verse continues by giving us a model for action that we should follow in our own lives: "And Jehoshaphat feared, and set himself to seek the LORD, and proclaimed a fast throughout all Judah" (v. 3). He then continued his response to fear by taking his place in the assembly of the people and leading them in praise—proclaiming who God was and all God had done for them. Read 2 Chronicles 20:12, and then describe the action that you commit to take to apply praise in your own life situations.

_____

_____

_____

3. God responded to Jehoshaphat and the people of Judah when they began to praise Him instead of cowering in fear before the enemy. Read verses 14 through 22, and describe how God responded. Then tell the rest of the story—what happened to the "great

multitude" that had threatened Jehoshaphat and the kingdom of Judah?

_____

_____

_____

Discover

> When you begin to develop a hunger for the deeper things of God, He will fill you. Hungry people are desperate people, and they are hungry for more of God than they ever had. Only Jesus satisfies that hunger!

What are some of the things you and your fellow church members can do to begin to praise God together for the needs and circumstances facing each other? Ideas you come up with may include:

- Setting aside at least one specific period of time for corporate fasting and prayer
- Creating an environment for praise by adding praise music to the times of prayer and intercession
- Meditating on specific praise portions of Scripture, such as Psalms
- Preparing "praise bookmarks" that can be given to members to use in their personal times of prayer

_____

_____

_____

Reflecting on what I learned

Where does the kind of faith come from that enables you to look to God and believe His Word no matter how grave your circumstances may *appear*? It is by hearing God's Word, by hearing the preaching of the gospel, that faith increases. There is something about getting in a church where the anointing flows and you hear the Word of God preached. Faith does not come from programs, dynamite worship teams, or being with a group of people who are like you. Faith comes when you hear a man or woman of God preach the Word without compromise to all who will listen. That is the birthplace of faith. If this revelation truly takes hold of your spirit, you will never allow the devil to talk you out of being faithful to God's house.

1. The longest psalm, Psalm 119, is all about the importance of immersing ourselves in the Word of God so our faith increases to believe God for the kinds of miracles we heard about in the DVD segment today. Psalm 119 is very specific about the benefits of God's Word. Look up each of the following verses, and describe the benefit named in each verse:

Verses 2–3

_____

_____

_____

Verse 11

_____

_____

_____

Verse 24

_____

_____

_____

Verses 25, 28

_____

_____

_____

Verse 36

_____

_____

_____

Verses 54–55

_____

_____

_____

Verse 66

_____

_____

_____

Verse 92

_____

_____

_____

Verses 97–98

_____

_____

_____

Verse 105

_____

_____

_____

Verse 130

_____

_____

_____

Verse 147

_____

_____

_____

Verse 171

_____

_____

_____

Let's pray about it

How I wish the body of Christ today had that same kind of hunger for God's Word. I would love to see the day when, if a Christian had to, he or she would go to church in pajamas rather than miss *hearing* God's Word! I know that sounds extreme, but we live in extreme times.

To begin your prayer today, pray the words of the verses from Psalm 119 you looked up just now:

> Blessed are those who keep His testimonies,
> Who seek Him with the whole heart!
> They also do no iniquity;
> They walk in His ways....
> Your word I have hidden in my heart,
> That I might not sin against You!...
> Your testimonies also are my delight
> And my counselors.
> My soul clings to the dust;
> Revive me according to Your word....
> My soul melts from heaviness;
> Strengthen me according to Your word....
> Incline my heart to Your testimonies,
> And not to covetousness....
> Your statutes have been my songs

In the house of my pilgrimage.
I remember Your name in the night, O Lord,
And I keep Your law....
Teach me good judgment and knowledge,
For I believe Your commandments....
Unless Your law had been my delight,
I would then have perished in my affliction....
Oh, how I love Your law!
It is my meditation all the day.
You, through Your commandments, make me wiser than
　　my enemies;
For they are ever with me....
Your word is a lamp to my feet
And a light to my path....
The entrance of Your words gives light;
It gives understanding to the simple....
I rise before the dawning of the morning,
And cry for help;
I hope in Your word....
My lips shall utter praise.
For You teach me Your statutes.

For your journey

> Too many Christians find that they are malnourished in the Word of God but well fed on the world, and they live defeated lives as a result. We must diligently feed on God's Word. Sometimes the best thing we can possibly do is starve our flesh and feed our spirit through a fast. Fasting helps you separate what you *want* from what you *need*. It causes you to focus on those things that really matter.

Digging deeper in God's Word

The eleventh chapter of the Book of Hebrews is often referred to as "the hall of faith," beginning with the words, "Now faith is the substance of things hoped for, the evidence of things not seen" (Heb. 11:1). Some of the most encouraging words in the Bible are found in this book.

1. Look up Hebrews 11, and complete the "faith-building" chart below about these *heroes of faith*:

Verse(s)	Hero of Faith	Faith Action Taken
4	Abel	
5	Enoch	
7	Noah	
8–9	Abraham	
11	Sarah	

17	Abraham	
18	Isaac	
21	Jacob	
22	Joseph	
23–29	Moses	
31	Rahab	

2. The Word of God and the record of God's faithfulness are the subject of all the beautiful songs of praise that David wrote. By reviewing the praise of David, we can be strengthened in the Word to push back the enemy and the negative situations and circumstances in our lives through praise. Read each of the following short praise psalms from David, and write how each one can help you to praise God in your situation.

   Psalm 3

   _____

   _____

   _____

Psalm 8

_____

_____

_____

Psalm 15

_____

_____

_____

Psalm 29

_____

_____

_____

Psalm 100

_____

_____

_____

Psalm 150

_____

_____

_____

My prayer journal

True worship that comes from our hearts feeds God and satisfies Him; it is something He desires—and deserves.

If you are using my twenty-one-day *Fasting Journal*, complete days 14 and 16 during your prayer journaling today. Or, on the lines below, journal the things that you have learned during this study session that will help you to learn to use God's Word to develop a greater "praise life" both in your times of personal study and prayer and to help your church body move to a new level of corporate prayer and praising.

_____

_____

_____

_____

_____

_____

_____

_____

_____

_____

_____

_____

_____

_____

_____

_____

But without faith it is impossible to please Him, for he who comes to God must believe that He is, and that He is a rewarder of those who diligently seek Him.

—HEBREWS 11:6—

Session Four

God's Priorities

That you may have a walk worthy of the Lord, fully pleasing Him, being fruitful in every good work and increasing in the knowledge of God; strengthened with all might, according to His glorious power, for all patience and longsuffering with joy; giving thanks to the Father who has qualified us to be partakers of the inheritance of the saints in the light.

—Colossians 1:10–12

Introduction

Questions to get you thinking

1. When you began your fast, you probably thought you knew just why you needed to fast. But as you moved into prayer, fasting, and reading God's Word, you probably became aware that God may have a different purpose for your fast. What are your priorities for your fast? What do you think are God's priorities?

My Priorities for My Fast	God's Priorities for My Fast
1.	1.
2.	2.
3.	3.

Play Session Four of the DVD

Notes from the DVD segment

Describe the Daniel fast.

_____

_____

_____

Michael's role as an archangel

_____

_____

_____

Gabriel's role as the messenger of God

_____

_____

_____

Fasting releases angelic forces

_____

_____

_____

New wineskins

_____

_____

_____

Fasting brings a brokenness into our spirit.

_____

_____

_____

DVD action points

> I am convinced that we will not walk in the perfect will of God until we seek Him through fasting. When you present your body in this manner, you open yourself up to hear from God. You will prove or discover His good and perfect will for your life.

1. First Thessalonians 4:3 tells us it is God's will for each of us to be sanctified. God doesn't want us to be different just to be different. He wants us to make a difference in our world, but if there is sin in our life, we cannot do that. What hidden sins keep you from being all God wants you to be? Will you allow God to sanctify you wholly and to anoint you to change your world for Him?

_____

_____

_____

2. Part of the process of being "transformed by the renewing of your mind" is the matter of getting rid of "old wineskins" and putting God's revelation into "new wineskins." What are the old wineskins that you have gotten rid of?

_____

_____

_____

What are the characteristics of your new wineskins?

_____

_____

_____

What God's Word tells us

God's weapons enable God's priorities to reign

God wants to equip us with the right weapons to be able to be victorious over the enemy and his attempts to pull us away from God by inflicting obstacles, hindrances, and negative circumstances upon our lives. Paul said the weapons of our warfare are "mighty through God to the pulling down of strong holds" (2 Cor. 10:4, KJV).

1. It was Paul who introduced us to *the weapons of our warfare*. Read Ephesians 6:10–20, where Paul describes the armor of God, and complete the chart below:

God's Armor Weapon	How You Can Use This Weapon in Your Life
1. Belt of truth	
2. Breastplate of righteousness	
3. Shoes of peace	
4. Shield of faith	
5. Helmet of salvation	
6. Sword of the Spirit	
7. Prayers of the Spirit	

2. I stressed the importance of being holy and identified *sanctification* as the process of becoming holy in daily life. It is by becoming holy that we are transformed by the renewing our minds. Then we can "prove what is that good and acceptable and perfect will of God" (Rom. 12:2). Sanctification involves these two things: being set apart from the world and sin and allowing the Holy Spirit to make us more like Jesus in what we do, think, and desire. To be like Jesus, we must understand what Jesus was like. Look up each of the following verses, and describe what characteristic they reveal about Jesus:

Matthew 4:19

_____

_____

_____

Matthew 20:27

_____

_____

_____

John 15:12

_____

_____

_____

Colossians 3:13

_____

_____

_____

3. Becoming Christlike also involves being so full of the Holy Spirit that we exhibit the fruit of the Spirit. Look up Galatians 5:22–23. Which of these fruit do you think others can see in your life?

_____

_____

_____

Which of these fruit do you need to develop in your life so that others can see it at work in your actions?

_____

_____

_____

Discover

The Holy Spirit will use your fast to reveal your true spiritual condition, resulting in brokenness, repentance, and a transformed life. God looks throughout the earth for those faithful few upon whom He can pour out His blessing in extraordinary ways. When you fast, you attract His attention as one willing to venture beyond the norms of religion and into the great adventure.

Reflecting on what I learned

By now, your fast has led you through many different emotions and levels of God's presence. You are beginning to see the reward of the humbling of your flesh that can only take place during a fast. You are dying to your own will and desires and sensing the desires of His heart filling you and prompting you to great things. Continue on this journey!

Take a few minutes today to reflect on this time of fasting and prayer that you are doing. How have you learned to "humble your flesh" so far? What selfish desires and actions have you learned to put to death? What are the godly desires and callings you sense God revealing to you?

_____

_____

_____

_____

_____

_____

_____

_____

_____

_____

Let's pray about it

Do not let the enemy drag you down with discouragement. Remember, God gives you the garment of praise for the spirit of heaviness. Sometimes you will not feel like praying when you are fasting, but pray anyway. You will be amazed how God will show up, and it will be like all of heaven has come down and glory has filled your soul.

During your prayer time today, pray aloud the prayer of Paul in Colossians 1:3–18. Insert your own name or "I" where indicated below:

> I give thanks to the God and Father of our Lord Jesus Christ, praying always for [*say your name*], that I may have faith in Christ Jesus and love for all the saints; because of the hope which is laid up for me in heaven, of which I have heard before in the word of the truth of the gospel, which has come to me, as it has also in all the world, and is bringing forth fruit, as it is also in my own life since the day I heard and knew the grace of God in truth....
>
> For this reason I also, since the day I heard it, do not cease to pray, and to ask that I may be filled with the knowledge of His will in all wisdom and spiritual understanding; that I may walk worthy of the Lord, fully pleasing Him, being fruitful in every good work and increasing in the knowledge of God; strengthened with all might, according to His glorious power, for all patience and longsuffering with joy; giving thanks to the Father who has qualified me to be a partaker of the inheritance of the saints in the light. He has delivered me from the power of darkness and conveyed me into the kingdom of the Son of His love, in whom I have redemption through His blood, the forgiveness of sins.

He is the image of the invisible God, the firstborn over all creation. For by Him all things were created that are in heaven and that are on earth, visible and invisible, whether thrones or dominions or principalities or powers. All things were created through Him and for Him. And He is before all things, and in Him all things consist. And He is the head of the body, the church, who is the beginning, the firstborn from the dead, that in all things He may have the preeminence.

—Adapted from Colossians 1:3–18

For your journey

Fasting, praying, and feeding on the Word of God puts that sword in your hand and positions you to discern the difference between your thoughts and God's thoughts. There is no higher authority than to know the heart of God for a situation you are facing.

Digging deeper in God's Word

As we feed on the Word of God, we will begin to understand what God's priorities for our lives—and for our times of fasting and prayer—really are.

1. Some of God's priorities are listed in the chart below. Read each Scripture passage, list God's priority in that scripture, and then tell what action you can take to put that priority to work in your life.

Scripture	God's Priority	My Life
Deuteronomy 6:7		
Proverbs 3:9		
Matthew 5:23		
Matthew 6:31–33		
Matthew 7:1–5		
Matthew 23:25–26		
Romans 8:13		
Revelation 2:4		

2. In Matthew 17:20, God tells us that we can move mountains with faith as small as a mustard seed. In chapter 12 of *Fasting*, I tell the story of planting a seed in the ground as a small boy and then pulling that seed out of the soil too soon, thus destroying the harvest. In this verse from Matthew, God describes our faith as a *seed*. We must learn that faith and patience go together. Just because we cannot see how God is rewarding our faith while we are in the middle of a crisis doesn't mean that nothing is happening—God is at work in the soil of our lives! In Matthew 17:14–19 we get the rest of the story—the disciples had tried to cast out the demon in the same boy that Jesus healed, and they had failed. When they asked Jesus why, He told them their faith

was too small—it was still a seed and was not ready to be harvested. Think of a time in your own life when you became impatient with God while waiting for Him to answer your prayers. Describe that time:

_____

_____

_____

Jesus put the emphasis on how *great our God is*, not on how great our faith is. Did you have your emphasis on your faith instead of on God? How would remembering the greatness of God have caused you to react differently in the situation you just described?

_____

_____

_____

3. An important revelation about God's priorities is revealed in Matthew 6:31–33. Read those verses. So many times our priorities cause us to worry and fret about the problems and challenges we face in our daily lives. Instead, we are told to "seek first his kingdom and his righteousness, and all these things will be given to you as well" (v. 33, NIV). On the lines below, list some of the things of this world that have caused you to worry and fret in the past. Beside each worry,

write a short prayer that seeks God's priorities about
that worry instead.

_____

_____

_____

_____

_____

_____

_____

_____

_____

_____

My prayer journal

If you want to please God, *believe* God. Take Him at His word.
When the apostle Paul was teaching the Corinthians, a knowledge-
seeking society, he told them, "We walk by faith, not by sight" (2 Cor.
5:7). Shadrach, Meshach, and Abed-nego walked by faith and not
by sight, saying, "Our God whom we serve is able to deliver us from

the burning fiery furnace, and He will deliver us from your hand, O king" (Dan. 3:17). Faith is the evidence of things unseen.

You are nearly through with this study guide about fasting. There is just one more DVD session where I will give instruction about fasting. You may also be nearly completed with the specific period of time that you committed to God for fasting and prayer. What is there in your heart that remains unfinished? What answers do you still need from God? What "worldly cares" are still clamoring for your attention? Where do you still need to be strengthened by the Word of God? On the lines below, journal where you are right now, today, and commit to "finishing the course" to victory.

_____

_____

_____

_____

_____

_____

_____

_____

_____

_____

_____

_____

_____

_____

_____

_____

_____

Now He who searches the hearts knows what the mind of the Spirit is, because He makes intercession for the saints according to the will of God. And we know that all things work together for good to those who love God, to those who are the called according to His purpose.

—ROMANS 8:27–28—

Session Five

Fasting Foundations

Therefore, brethren, be even more diligent to make your call and election sure, for if you do these things you will never stumble; for so an entrance will be supplied to you abundantly into the everlasting kingdom of our Lord and Savior Jesus Christ.

—2 Peter 1:10–11

Introduction

Questions to get you thinking

1. Is there any unforgiveness, bitterness, or other hindrances that you have yet to lay fully before your Lord?

   _____

   _____

   _____

2. How will you prepare for the blessing, harvest, and anointing you are about to experience?

   _____

   _____

   _____

Play Session Five of the DVD

Notes from the DVD segment

When you fast and pray, you will draw closer to the Lord.

_____

_____

_____

Fasting is emptying what you have to receive what God has.

_____

_____

_____

Fasting is crucifying King Stomach.

_____

_____

_____

Fasting is tasting the Bread of Heaven.

_____

_____

_____

Fasting is waiting before the Lord.

_____

_____

_____

Fasting is drinking the Living Water.

_____

_____

_____

Fasting is being led by the Holy Spirit.

_____

_____

Fasting is resting in the Lord.

_____

_____

_____

DVD action points

> Fasting will bring you into destiny. Fasting will bring you into alignment with God's plan for your life. Now is the time to fast, to seek God diligently, to sanctify yourself, to discern God's priorities, and to walk in His promises. *Go for it!*

1. The Holy Spirit is looking for empty vessels into which He can pour His oil and anointing. In 2 Kings 4:1–7, as long as the woman had empty vessels, her oil did not run out and her needs were met. What do you need to empty in your life so you have empty vessels into which God can pour His anointing and blessing?

   _____

   _____

   _____

2. Judges 3:17–22 tells the story of Ehud and Eglon and describes the dirt that flowed out of Eglon's belly. I used DIRT as an acrostic. Can you list what each letter stands for?

   • D

   _____

   _____

- I

_____

_____

- R

_____

_____

- T[1]

_____

_____

What dirt needs to leave your life?

_____

_____

_____

What God's Word tells us

Is your blade sharp enough?

Can you imagine having an extended conversation with one of the higher-ranking angels of God? Suppose that angel came to you and told you of kingdoms that would rise and fall in coming years, even

---

1 Answers to DIRT acrostic: Disobedience, Ignorance, Rebellion, Temperament or Tongue.

explaining what principalities would manipulate those leaders and how alliances would form and be crushed as new kings rose to power. I'd be willing to give up a Twinkie or a T-bone steak for a few weeks in order to have my spirit open enough to receive such a visitation!

1. When Daniel was taken captive to Babylon and chosen along with three friends to be trained in the ways of the Chaldeans to eventually become personal assistants of the king, he refused to defile himself with the foods of the palace. (See Daniel 1.) Read Daniel 1:17, and tell how God honored the stand Daniel took to focus on God's priorities and instructions.

    _____

    _____

    _____

2. At the end of Daniel's life, once again he took a stand by entering a time of fasting (Dan. 10:2–3). Read Daniel 10:1–19. What happened as a result of Daniel's fast?

    _____

    _____

    _____

What did the angel tell Daniel (v. 12)?

_____

_____

_____

Daniel's prayers had been heard in heaven from the very first day he started the fast! How does this encourage you about the prayers you have been praying during your fast?

_____

_____

_____

3. Before the angel appeared to Daniel in Daniel 10, Daniel prayed a very specific prayer. Read Daniel's prayer in Daniel 9:3–19. Daniel understood why disaster had befallen his people: "We have sinned and committed iniquity, we have done wickedly and rebelled, even by departing from Your precepts and Your judgments" (v. 5). Can you see the parallels to the people in Daniel's day? America is rapidly becoming a pagan nation. Our only hope is to humble ourselves in fasting and prayer. Using Daniel's prayer as your guide, write your own prayer for America on the lines below:

_____

_____

_____

Discover

> We can humble ourselves and pray and seek His face and
> expect Him to hear from heaven and heal our land
> (2 Chron. 7:14). He heard Daniel on the very first day!

Reflecting on what I learned

Fasting is not a means to promote yourself. The greatest thing fasting will do for you will be to break down all of the stuff that accumulates from this world that blocks you from clear communion with the Father.

1. In *Fasting*, I say, "Some of the greatest miracles, breakthroughs, and seasons of prayer I have ever experienced did not come when I was 'feeling led' to pray and fast. They actually came when the last thing I wanted to do was drag myself to my prayer place, but I did, and God honored my faithfulness." When you began this time of fasting and prayer and began working your way through this study guide, you may have felt like saying, "Where He drags me I will wallow, and what He feeds me I will swallow," rather than, "Where He leads me I will follow." Take some time to reflect

on how your perspective of fasting and prayer has changed during this time. Describe your experience on the lines below.

_____

_____

_____

Let's pray about it

If you let it, your flesh will take over and rule your life. That is why times of fasting are so crucial to your walk with God. Fasting helps you establish dominion and authority over your flesh.

During your prayer time today, begin by praying aloud 2 Chronicles 7:14–15:

> If My people who are called by My name will humble themselves, and pray and seek My face, and turn from their wicked ways, then I will hear from heaven, and will forgive their sin and heal their land. Now My eyes will be open and My ears attentive to prayer made in this place.

Then enter a time of praising God in your prayers for the victories, revelations, and lessons you have learned during this season of prayer and fasting.

_____

_____

_____

For your journey

> By now you are so sensitive to the Holy Spirit that you
> realize nothing else will satisfy. Nothing else will do in
> a world gone mad. This world needs the touch of God.
> It needs the sweeping movement of the Holy Spirit
> convicting men of sin and drawing them to the cross. But
> you have to hunger for it. You have to thirst for it. There's
> a difference between wanting a drink and being thirsty.
> When you're thirsty, everything in you says, "I've got to have
> it." And when you get thirsty, He'll pour out His Spirit.

Digging deeper in God's Word

Battles will rage long after you have completed your fast. Some things you lay hold of during the fast will require further diligence to see victory. To help you "stay the course" in the days after your fast—and throughout the year—remember the following twelve steps to victory. (Adapted from pages 105–106 of the *Fasting Journal*.)

Read the scriptures for each step, and write down how each one applies to your life.

1. Make it hard on God and easy on you. Take the pressure off yourself to make things happen, because that's God's job (Matt. 11:28; John 5:40; 6:29).

_____

_____

_____

2. Keep on swinging. Don't settle for partial victory (2 Tim. 4:7–8).

_____

_____

_____

3. God says, "When you approach a door that is very large, do not fear, because I will open it." When God opens the door, no man can shut it (Rev. 3:7–8).

_____

_____

_____

4. Don't move in the dark. If you don't know God's will, don't move (Exod. 14:13; Ruth 3:18; Ps. 46:10).

_____

_____

_____

5. Be strong and very courageous. If you lack courage, pray (Phil. 4:6–7).

_____

_____

_____

6. Don't do anything until you ask the Lord first. He will give you a clear word (Eph. 2:10).

_____

_____

_____

7. Don't ask how much it costs; ask God if He wants it done. If so, He'll take care of the cost (2 Cor. 9:8; 3 John 2).

_____

_____

_____

8. Be patient. God loves the last-minute save! "Whoever believes will not act hastily" (Isa. 28:16).

_____

_____

_____

9. Don't stick to sensible methods. If the Lord tells you to do something, do it (Prov. 3:5–6; Isa. 25:3–4)!

_____

_____

_____

10. Practice the John the Baptist factor: "He must increase, but I must decrease" (John 3:30; Phil. 1:21).

_____

_____

_____

11. Look out! You haven't seen anything yet when you mix faith with the Word of God (Hab. 2:4; Rom. 10:17).

_____

_____

_____

12. P-U-S-H: Pray Until Something Happens *or* Praise Until Something Happens (Ps. 149; 2 Chron. 20:21–22; Heb. 13:15).

_____

_____

_____

My prayer journal

In Luke 15 we read the story of the prodigal son. This story is a symbol of people in your world who are lost in sin and need to discover the redemption and hope that can only be found in Jesus Christ. A challenge for you as you end this five-week study of fasting is to find ways to share with others the rewards that God is bringing into your life as a result of your fast. Your journey through this process has, no doubt, taken you places you have never been and hopefully brought you into a place of incredible blessing. Your story matters. God has done a wonderful thing for you, and the challenge now is to take what He has done and multiply it into the lives of others. Many will be encouraged and strengthened through your story of faithfulness and by the testimony of your experiences. Prayerfully consider what you would be willing to share with others.

On the lines below, list five people who you know need to hear your story of God's blessings and healing in your life. Beside each name, describe how and when you plan to share your story with that person.

_____

_____

_____

_____

_____

_____

_____

_____

_____

_____

If you extend your soul to the hungry
And satisfy the afflicted soul,
Then your light shall dawn in the darkness,
And your darkness shall be as the noonday.
The LORD will guide you continually,
And satisfy your soul in drought,
And strengthen your bones;
You shall be like a watered garden,
And like a spring of water, whose waters do not fall.
Those from among you
Shall build the old waste places;
You shall raise up the foundations of many generations;
And you shall be called the Repairer of the Breach,
The Restorer of Streets to Dwell In.
—ISAIAH 58:10–12—

Personal Reflection

Personal Reflection

_____

_____

_____

_____

_____

_____

_____

_____

_____

_____

_____

_____

_____

_____

_____

_____

_____

_____

_____

_____

_____

_____

_____

_____

_____

_____

_____